JUL 1 2 2018

HOW-TO LIBRARY

CRAFTING WITH RECYCLABLES: EVEN MORE PROJECTS

By Dana Meachen Rau • Illustrated by Kathleen Petelinsek

CHERRY LAKE PUBLISHING • ANN ARBOR, MICHIGAN

Published in the United States of America by Cherry Lake Publishing
Ann Arbor, Michigan
www.cherrylakepublishing.com

Photo Credits: Pages 4 and 5, ©Huguette Roe/Shutterstock; page 6, ©vipman/Shutterstock; page 7, ©spwidoff/Shutterstock; page 14, ©Dana Meachen Rau; page 29, ©Volt Collection/Shutterstock; page 32, ©Charlie Rau.

Library of Congress Cataloging-in-Publication Data
Names: Rau, Dana Meachen, 1971– author.
Title: Crafting with recyclables : even more projects / by Dana Meachen Rau.
Other titles: How-to library.
Description: Ann Arbor, Michigan : Cherry Lake Publishing, 2016. | 2016 | Series: How-to library | Series: Crafts | Audience: Grades 4 to 6.
Identifiers: LCCN 2015049442| ISBN 9781634714198 (lib. bdg.) | ISBN 9781634714358 (pbk.) | ISBN 9781634714273 (pdf) | ISBN 9781634714433 (ebook)
Subjects: LCSH: Handicraft—Juvenile literature. | Recycling (Waste, etc.)—Juvenile literature.
Classification: LCC TT171 .R38 2016 | DDC 745.5—dc23 LC record available at http://lccn.loc.gov/2015049442

Cherry Lake Publishing would like to acknowledge the work of the Partnership for 21st Century Learning. Please visit *www.p21.org* for more information.

Printed in the United States of America
Corporate Graphics
July 2016

HOW-TO LIBRARY

TABLE OF CONTENTS

Out of the Blue Bin...4

Upcycling...6

Basic Supplies...8

Painting Tips...10

Sewing Tips...11

Faux Leather Vase...12

T-Shirt Infinity Scarf...14

Snazzy Desk Shelves...16

Jelly Jar Snow Globe...18

Metal Friends...20

Pants Pockets...22

Sidesplitting Bookends...24

Glowing Plastic Bottle Lamp...26

Ordinary to Extraordinary...29

Glossary...30
For More Information...31
Index...32
About the Author...32

Out of the Blue Bin

At landfills, bulldozers are used to pack in as much trash as possible.

Have you ever seen a landfill? A landfill is an area of land set aside for dumping trash. The trash is buried and covered with soil. As people throw away more and more trash, more land is turned into landfills. But we don't want a world full of garbage! To stop this, we need to reduce the amount of trash we make.

Recycling is a great way to make less trash. This is the process of turning old materials into new ones. Paper, plastic, metal, and glass are all recyclable materials.

The symbol for recycling is a triangle made of arrows. You may have seen it on the side of large blue bins. Many towns and cities provide these bins for households as part of their recycling programs. Trucks collect recyclable materials from the bins. They bring these materials to a recycling center instead of a landfill.

What happens at a recycling center? Machines sort the recyclable materials. They are then **processed** and remade into new paper, plastic, metal, and glass items.

This kind of recycling isn't the only way to reduce the amount of trash we create. Read on to see how you can recycle materials into art or other useful items yourself!

Recyclable materials such as aluminum cans are pressed together into bales at recycling centers.

Upcycling

Do you have old clothes you don't wear anymore?
Upcycle them!

Recycled materials need to be shredded, melted, or processed some other way before they are made into new things. But you can recycle at home in a simpler way. You can transform recyclable materials by upcycling them.

To upcycle means to change an item into something even better. For example, you can transform an old T-shirt into a fashionable new scarf. Or you can turn empty cardboard boxes into a useful set of shelves. All you need are recyclable materials, craft supplies, and your own creativity.

Make something for yourself or create gifts for friends and family. You might not even need to spend any money for supplies. You probably have most of them in your home already.

With upcycling, you can change unwanted things such as aluminum cans, plastic water bottles, or old magazines into stuff everyone will want. Let's get started transforming the ordinary into the extraordinary!

Start by gathering clean bottles and cans to use in your projects.

Basic Supplies

You might have most of these supplies at home already! Recyclable supplies should be especially easy to find.

Recyclable Supplies

- Glass bottles and jars
- Plastic bottles
- Tin cans
- Magazines
- Cardboard boxes

Supplies for Holding Things Together

- *Clear tacky glue* is very sticky and strong.
- *A hot glue gun* heats sticks of glue until they melt. The melted glue forms a solid seal when it dries. Always ask for help from an adult when using a glue gun. The glue gets very hot and can cause burns.
- *Waterproof glue* can be purchased in hardware stores, craft stores, or aquarium supply stores.
- *Masking tape* is a light brown or off-white color.
- *Washi tape* is a decorative tape that you can find at craft stores.

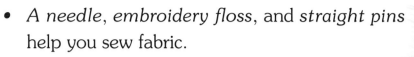

- *A needle, embroidery floss,* and *straight pins* help you sew fabric.
- *Binder clips* hold boxes in place.

Cutting Tools

- *Scissors* for cutting paper
- *A box cutter* for cutting plastic (Always ask an adult for help when using a box cutter. It is very sharp.)
- *Fabric scissors* for cutting cloth

Craft and Office Supplies

- Water-based acrylic paint
- Water-based varnish
- Paintbrushes and sponge brushes
- Ruler
- Glitter
- Ribbon

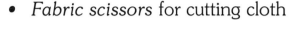

Other Supplies

- Plastic game pieces, small toys, flowers, beads, or other decorations
- Old clothes, such as T-shirts and jeans
- Small hardware, such as nails, screws, nuts, and bolts
- Holiday lights
- Marbles or small stones

Painting Tips

You will need to use paint for some of the projects in this book. Here are some tips to keep things neat and easy!

- Cover your work surface with newspaper before you get started. You can also wear an apron or smock to protect your clothes.
- Use water-based acrylic paint and varnish. When these are still wet, they wash off of brushes and other surfaces easily with soap and water.
- You can use a paintbrush when you need to paint small areas. A sponge brush is useful for larger areas.
- Use a paper plate as a **palette** to hold your paint. Keep a container of water nearby to rinse out your brush between colors. Also, keep a paper towel handy to blot your brush or clean up spills.

Sewing Tips

Sewing something new from old material is a great way to upcycle clothing and fabric. Here are some basic sewing skills to learn.

- To thread a needle, hold it steady and poke the thread through the needle's **eye**. Pull the thread through until the two loose ends meet. Knot them together. If you have trouble threading a needle with thick embroidery floss, you can separate the strands and use less floss.

- To sew a running stitch, poke your needle up through the fabric. Pull it all the way through until it stops at the knot. Then poke the needle down into the fabric close to where it came up. Pull it all the way through the other side. Repeat, sewing stitches in as straight a line as you can, until you reach the end of your work.

- Now you need to secure the end of the thread. On the back of your work, poke the needle in and out again very close together, but don't pull the thread all the way through. Instead, poke the needle through the loop made by the thread, then pull it tight. Repeat to make a double knot. Use fabric scissors to trim off the extra thread.

Faux Leather Vase

Faux means fake. Faux finishes can make one type of material look like another. In this project, you will make a glass bottle look like it is made of leather! Tuck in some dried flowers to make an attractive display.

Materials

- Masking tape
- Glass bottle, any size, cleaned and dried well
- Brown acrylic paint
- Paper plate palette
- Sponge brushes
- Soft cloth
- Varnish

Steps

1. Rip off a small piece of masking tape. Place it on the side of the bottle. Press it flat to get out any air bubbles.
2. Place another piece of tape on the bottle, slightly overlapping the first. Continue overlapping pieces of tape until the entire bottle is covered. Be sure to cover the bottom and around the top rim.

3. Squeeze some brown paint onto your palette. Use a sponge brush to paint a small area of the bottle.

4. Immediately wipe the paint off with the soft cloth. Wipe carefully so you don't lift up the edges of the tape.

5. Continue to paint small areas and wipe them off gently until you have painted the whole bottle. Let the bottle dry for about an hour.

6. Squeeze some varnish onto your palette and use a sponge brush to apply it all over the bottle. Let the varnish dry completely.

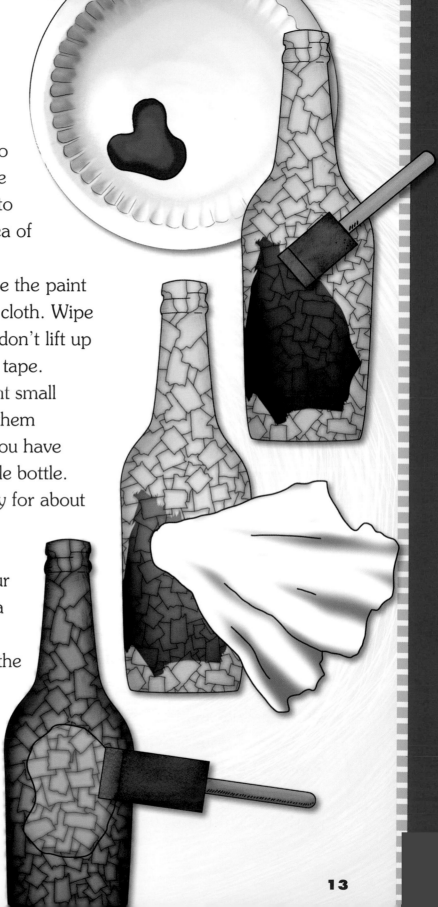

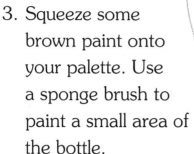

WATER BASED

Polycrylic

T-Shirt Infinity Scarf

Do you have T-shirts that don't fit anymore? Or ones that are too worn-out to wear? You can transform them into a soft and stylish **accessory** for any outfit.

Materials
- 3 T-shirts (referred to below as Shirt A, Shirt B, and Shirt C)
- Ruler
- Fabric scissors

Steps
1. Measure 1 inch (2.5 centimeters) from the bottom of Shirt A (including the **hem** in the measure), and cut it off all the way around. This will be the base of your scarf. Open it into a loop. Don't worry if it doesn't look long enough. The fabric will stretch as you work.

2. Cut the rest of Shirt A into three equal pieces. Then cut each of these sections into strips about 1 inch (2.5 cm) wide. You won't get as many strips from the top section. Just cut out as many as you can between the neck and the sleeves.

3. Repeat steps 1 and 2 on Shirt B and Shirt C. You can **discard** their bottom hem strips.

4. Tie one of the strips in a tight knot onto the loop. Tie another strip right next to it. Continue tying strips around the loop as closely together as possible.

5. You are done when you complete the loop! To wear the scarf, you can let it hang around your neck in one long loop or you can loop it around a second time.

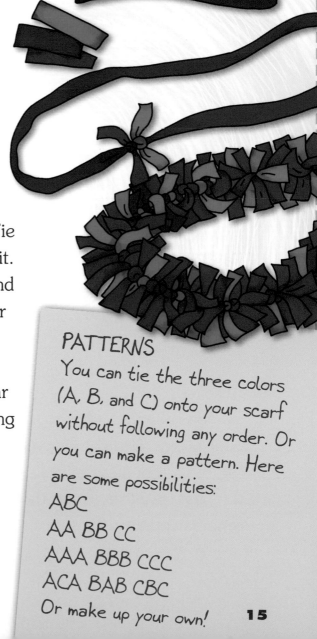

PATTERNS
You can tie the three colors (A, B, and C) onto your scarf without following any order. Or you can make a pattern. Here are some possibilities:

ABC

AA BB CC

AAA BBB CCC

ACA BAB CBC

Or make up your own!

Snazzy Desk Shelves

Keep your desk neat and organized! Transform shoe boxes and smaller gift boxes into a set of cubbies to display and hold little items.

Materials

- Boxes in various sizes (shoe box size and smaller)
- Clear tacky glue
- Binder clips
- White acrylic paint and a variety of other colors
- Paper plate palette
- Paintbrush or sponge brush

Steps

1. Decide how you want to arrange your boxes. Use the biggest box as the base. Then experiment with the best way to arrange the others around it.

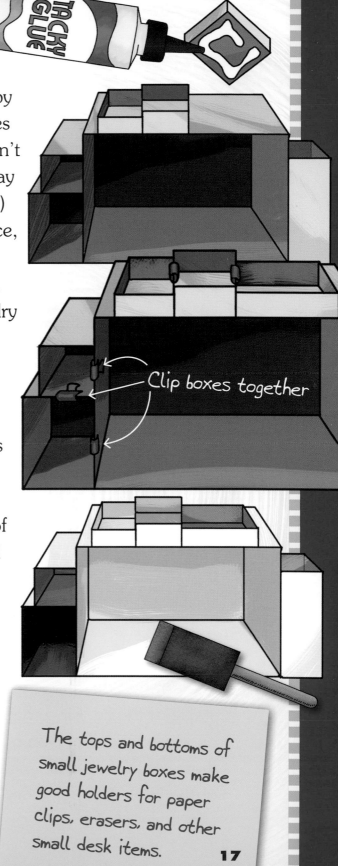

2. Glue the boxes together one by one. Make sure the front edges of the boxes are lined up. (Don't worry about the back—it's okay if some of the boxes stick out.)

3. When all the boxes are in place, secure **adjacent** boxes with binder clips to help hold them tightly together. Let the glue dry completely for a few hours.

4. Remove the clips. Paint the outside and back of all the boxes with white paint. You don't need to paint the insides or the bottoms. Let the paint dry completely. If your boxes are a dark color or have lots of words to cover, you may need to paint a second coat.

5. Paint the insides of the boxes with a **contrasting** color or colors. Let them dry completely. Paint a second coat if needed.

6. Fill the cubbies of your shelves with all sorts of fun stuff!

Clip boxes together

The tops and bottoms of small jewelry boxes make good holders for paper clips, erasers, and other small desk items.

17

Jelly Jar Snow Globe

Some people collect snow globes when they visit new places on vacation. You can make your own collection out of glass jars and old plastic toys.

Materials

- Plastic game pieces, small toys, flowers, beads, or other decorations
- A jelly jar and lid
- Waterproof glue
- Water
- Measuring spoons
- Glitter
- Ribbon

Steps

1. Collect your plastic decorations and arrange them on the inside of the lid. Glue them on piece by piece. Don't glue them too close to the edges of the lid. Let the glue dry.

(Check the instructions on the glue package to find out how long it needs to dry to become waterproof.)

2. Fill the jar about ¾ full of water. Add ½ teaspoon of glitter and stir it up.

3. Place the lid with decorations onto the jar. Screw it on tightly. Flip the jar over and shake it gently to test it. Decide if it needs a little more water or glitter. If so, unscrew the lid and add them.

4. When you are happy with the amounts of water and glitter, glue around the inside of the lid. Screw it tightly to secure it. Let it dry completely.

5. Tie a ribbon around the lid and secure it with a bow. Then flip the jar over to enjoy the gently falling snow!

Metal Friends

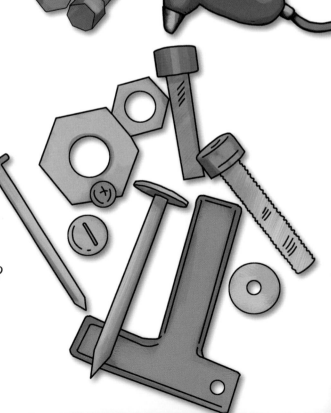

Look in drawers, a toolbox, or anywhere else you or members of your family might stash extra screws, nails, washers, handles, or other hardware. Find ways to combine them into a whole cast of characters or critters! There is no right or wrong way to do this project. Let the different types of hardware **inspire** your creations.

Materials

- Nails, screws, nuts, bolts, and other metal hardware
- Hot glue gun

Steps

1. Collect your materials and lay them out on your workspace. Experiment with the pieces. Do any look like eyes? Is there something that would make a good body or base? Arms? Legs? Wings?

Try different combinations until you find an arrangement you like.

2. Use the hot glue gun to attach the pieces to each other. Create a zoo of animals, a group of rock stars, or the members of your family. Above all, have fun!

Ask an adult to help you with the hot glue gun. It gets very hot and can burn you.

Pants Pockets

Turn old jeans into a handy holder for stuffed animals, craft supplies, nail polish, small toys, or anything else that you want to keep safe in a pocket!

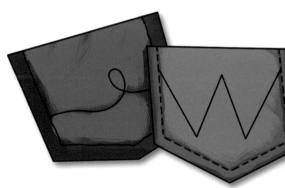

Materials

- Two old pairs of jeans
- Fabric scissors
- Embroidery floss
- Sewing needle
- Straight pins

Steps

1. Cut the back pockets from the jeans around their sewn edges. Then cut the fabric off the back of the pockets.
2. Cut along the outer leg seam on one of the pairs of jeans. Then cut across to the area where the two legs meet. Finally, cut down the inner leg seam. You will end up with a long, rectangular piece of fabric.

3. Cut off the waistband of one of the pairs of jeans. With the button or snap at the top, trim the ends to about 8 inches (20.3 cm) long.

4. Fold over the top of the leg fabric about 1 inch (2.5 cm). Pin the ends of the waistband to each corner of the leg piece. Sew them in place with a running stitch.

5. Place the four pockets on the leg piece. Pin them in place.

6. Starting in the top corner of a pocket, sew down the side, across the bottom, and up the other side to secure it. Don't sew across the top. Repeat with the other three pockets.

Sidesplitting Bookends

Two tin cans and an old magazine can turn into fun supports for your books in this simple project. They can even hold bookmarks so they are nearby when you need them! Try to choose a **symmetrical** picture. A face, a flower blossom, or a baseball are all good choices.

Materials

- Pages from a magazine with lots of words
- Varnish
- Paper plate palette
- Sponge brush
- 2 tin cans of the same size, labels removed; cleaned and dried well
- A picture from a magazine
- Felt
- Marker
- Clear tacky glue
- Marbles or small stones

Steps

1. Tear the word pages from the magazine into small pieces.
2. Squeeze varnish on your palette. Use the sponge brush to apply the varnish to a small area on one can. Place a piece of torn magazine onto the wet area. Then paint over the piece with more varnish.

3. Continue painting, placing, and repainting pieces of magazine with varnish until the entire surface is covered. Repeat with the other can. Let them dry for about an hour.

4. Cut the magazine picture in half. Cut out any extra space around your image.

5. Apply more varnish to the surface of one of the cans. Place half of your image onto the can, then paint over it with more varnish. Repeat with the other half of the image on the other can. Make sure the images are straight and lined up with each other.

6. Place the cans on the felt and trace around the bottom of each one with a marker. Cut out the felt circles. Glue them to the bottom of each can with tacky glue. Let both the varnish and glue dry completely.

7. Flip the cans over and fill each about halfway with marbles or stones. Place them on each end of a bunch of books!

DECOUPAGE

Decoupage is the art of gluing paper onto a surface with varnish. You can decoupage with all sorts of paper. However, thin paper, such as magazine pages or tissue paper, works best—especially when it needs to bend around an uneven surface.

Glowing Plastic Bottle Lamp

If you drink a lot of bottled water, you may notice all those empty bottles piling up. You can use them as building supplies to create a standing lamp that will brighten up your room.

Materials

- 35 water bottles
- Hot glue gun
- Washi tape
- Scissors or box cutter
- 50-light strand of LED holiday lights

Steps

1. The lamp will be made up of five units of seven bottles each. To build a unit, start by cutting off the top and bottom of one bottle so you have a tube shape. This will be the center of the unit.
2. Glue a bottle to each side of this tube. Make sure it sits level on your work surface.

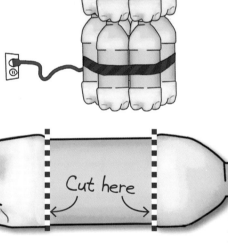

Cut here

Glue here

Ask an adult to help you with the box cutter and hot glue gun.

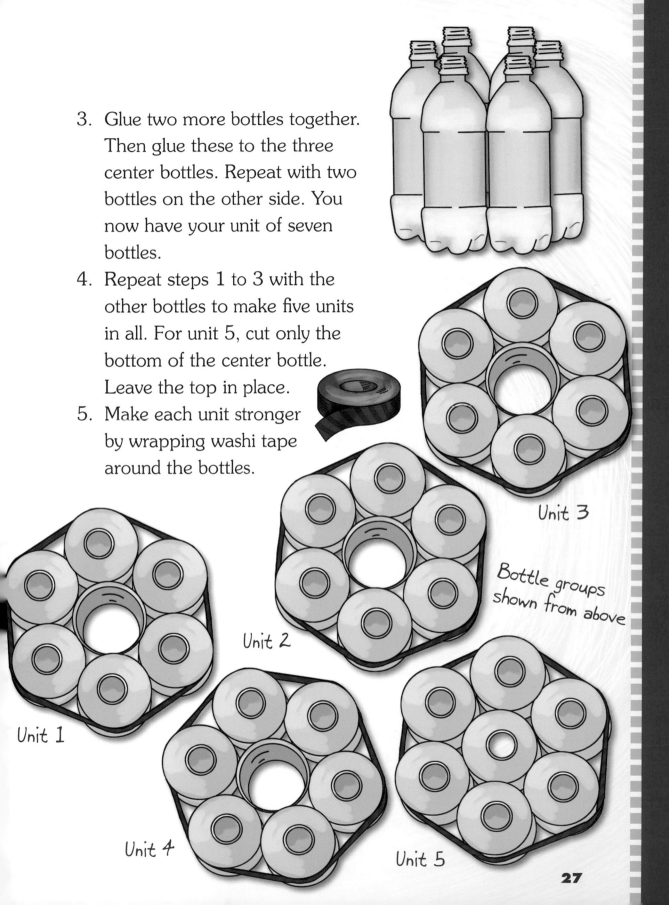

3. Glue two more bottles together. Then glue these to the three center bottles. Repeat with two bottles on the other side. You now have your unit of seven bottles.

4. Repeat steps 1 to 3 with the other bottles to make five units in all. For unit 5, cut only the bottom of the center bottle. Leave the top in place.

5. Make each unit stronger by wrapping washi tape around the bottles.

Unit 3

Bottle groups shown from above

Unit 2

Unit 1

Unit 4

Unit 5

27

6. Next, you are going to thread your units onto the string of lights like beads on a necklace. Start by holding the outlet end of the lights. Thread it through the center tube of units 1, 2, 3, and 4. When you get to unit 5, stuff the outlet and about 10 lights into the underside of the center bottle.

7. You are now going to start gluing the units together. Place unit 5 mouth-side down on your work surface. Squeeze glue onto the bottoms of the bottles and place the mouths of the unit 4 bottles on top. Press down so the bottles stick to each other.

8. Stuff another 10 lights of the strand into the center tube of unit 4. Then repeat step 7. Continue with unit 3, unit 2, and unit 1, until you have an upside-down tower of 5 units.

9. Cut a notch into the edge of the center tube of unit 1. Secure the strand of lights in this notch, leaving enough hanging out to reach the nearest electrical outlet.

10. Flip your lamp right-side up. Plug it in and let it glow!

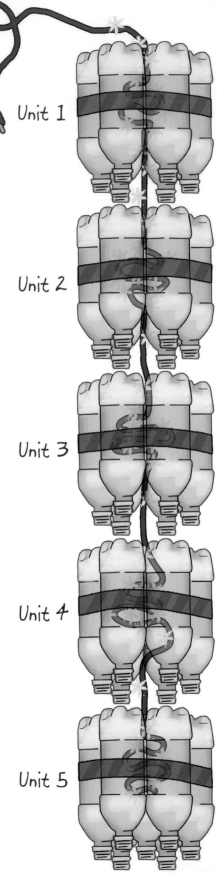

Unit 1

Unit 2

Unit 3

Unit 4

Unit 5

Ordinary to Extraordinary

Creative people have big imaginations. When you work with recyclable materials and upcycle them into something new, you are using your *reimagination*!

Have a reimagination brainstorm! Divide up a big piece of paper into four categories: paper, metal, glass, and plastic. Get a group of friends together to help you think of ideas to fill each space. You probably have a lot of great ideas on your own. Imagine how many you will have if you work together!

You can transform trash into fun and useful items. Reimagine the ordinary as something extraordinary!

Your home recycling bins are full of possibilities!

Glossary

accessory (ak-SES-ur-ee) a small item worn with clothes

adjacent (uh-JAY-suhnt) next to each other

contrasting (KAHN-tras-ting) very different

discard (dis-KARD) throw away

eye (EYE) the hole at one end of a sewing needle

hem (HEM) an edge of fabric that has been folded and sewn down

inspire (in-SPIRE) to spark a creative idea

palette (PAL-it) a flat board for holding and mixing paints

processed (PRAH-sest) prepared or changed by a series of steps

recycling (ree-SYE-kling) the process of turning old items, such as glass, plastic, paper, and metal, into new products

symmetrical (si-MET-ri-kuhl) exactly the same on both sides of a center line

For More Information

Books

Edgar, David, and Robin A. Edgar. *Fantastic Recycled Plastic: 30 Clever Creations to Spark Your Imagination*. New York: Lark Books, 2009.

Martin, Laura C. *Recycled Crafts Box*. North Adams, MA: Storey Kids, 2003.

Rau, Dana Meachen. *Glass*. New York: Marshall Cavendish Benchmark, 2012.

Sirrine, Carol. *Cool Crafts with Old Wrappers, Cans, and Bottles*. Mankato, MN: Capstone Press, 2010.

Web Sites

Environmental Protection Agency: Recycle City

www.epa.gov/recyclecity

Learn about the many ways a community can cut down on landfill waste.

Free Kids Crafts: Recycled Crafts

www.freekidscrafts.com/recycled-crafts

Check out lots of ideas for crafts made out of recycled materials.

Recyclart

www.recyclart.org

Browse the beautiful art people have created by upcycling.

Index

brainstorming, 29

craft supplies, 9
cutting tools, 9

decoupage, 25

Faux Leather Vase project, 12–13

glass, 4, 5, 8
Glowing Plastic Bottle Lamp project,
    26–28

hot glue guns, 8, 21, 26

ideas, 29

Jelly Jar Snow Globe project, 18–19

landfills, 4

masking tape, 8
metal, 4, 5, 8
Metal Friends project, 20–21

office supplies, 9

painting, 10
Pants Pockets project, 22–23
paper, 4, 5, 8
plastic, 4, 5, 8
processing, 5

recycling bins, 5
recycling centers, 5
recycling symbol, 5
running stitches, 11

safety, 8, 9, 21, 26
sewing, 11
Sidesplitting Bookends project, 24–25
Snazzy Desk Shelves project, 16–17
supplies, 8–9

tacky glue, 8
tape, 8
trash, 4
T-Shirt Infinity Scarf project, 14–15

upcycling, 6–7

washi tape, 8
waterproof glue, 8

About the Author

Dana Meachen Rau is the author of more than 300 books for children on many topics, including science, history, cooking, and crafts. She creates, experiments, researches, and writes from her home office in Burlington, Connecticut.